IR

DISCARD

Rockets

Peak Performance

Sports Nutrition

Donna Shryer
with Jodi Forschmiedt

Marshall Cavendish
Benchmark
New York

Marshall Cavendish Benchmark
99 White Plains Road
Tarrytown, NY 10591
www.marshallcavendish.us

Library of Congress Cataloging-in-Publication Data

Shryer, Donna.
    Peak performance : sports nutrition / by Donna Shryer with Jodi Forschmiedt.
        p. cm. — (Benchmark rockets : food and you)
    Includes index.
    Summary: "An introduction to nutrition for athletes. Explains how adding
excellent nutrition to training programs will help an athlete's performance"—
Provided by publisher.
    ISBN 978-0-7614-4366-7
    1. Athletes—Nutrition—Juvenile literature. 2. Physical fitness—Nutritional
aspects—Juvenile literature. I. Forschmiedt, Jodi. II. Title.

TX361.A8S52 2009
613.2'024796—dc22
2008054285

Publisher: Michelle Bisson
Editorial Development and Book Design: Trillium Publishing, Inc.

Photo research by Trillium Publishing, Inc.

Cover photo: iStockphoto.com/Michel de Nijs

The photographs and illustrations in this book are used by permission and
through the courtesy of: iStockphoto.com: Brandon Clark, 1, 21; Tor Lindqvist,
14. Shutterstock.com: iofoto, 3; Noam Armonn, 8; Larry St. Pierre, 10; Oguz Aral,
15; Kathy Burns-Millyard, 18; Edyta Pawlowska, 19. Jupiterimages Corporation: 4.
USDA: 6, 7. age fotostock: Raymond Forbes, 24.

Printed in Malaysia
1 3 5 6 4 2

Contents

1 The Nutrition Team

You have top-of-the-line shoes. Your coach demands great form. You train hard every day. Yet it's all for nothing without the right fuel for your body. Where does the fuel come from? It comes from food!

Your body breaks up food into **nutrients**. Nutrients are absorbed and used in many ways:

- To get energy
- To repair wear and tear
- To help you grow
- To keep your body processes working smoothly
- To fight illness and infection

All of the nutrients work together to keep you healthy. Even if only one important nutrient is missing, many systems in your body may stop working properly.

Nutrients to Go

Your body needs larger amounts of some nutrients. They include **carbohydrates**, fat, **protein**, and water. Other nutrients are needed in smaller amounts. These nutrients are **vitamins** and **minerals**.

You need to feed yourself enough nutrients every day. You can get carbohydrates from foods made with grains. Carbohydrates also come from fruits, vegetables, soy, and dairy products. You get **fiber**, which is technically a carbohydrate, from plant foods. Your body can't digest fiber, but you need plenty of it.

Unsaturated fat is healthy and necessary. You get unsaturated fat from most vegetable oils, some fish, nuts, seeds, olives, and avocados. You get protein from meat, soy, beans, nuts, eggs, and seeds.

Carbohydrates, fat, and protein provide your body with energy. A **calorie** is a unit of measurement for energy, just like a foot or meter is a unit of measurement for distance. If you are an athlete, you use a lot of energy every day. You need to make sure you are getting the right amount of calories for your body.

Water does not provide energy, yet your body needs a lot of water. Your body wouldn't function at all without it. Vitamins and minerals do not provide calories either, but you must have them to get energy from food. You can get all the vitamins and minerals your body needs from a healthy, balanced diet.

Nutrition Officials

Your teammates might give you advice about nutrition, but they may not have their facts straight. You need to know how many calories and nutrients your body requires. It is important to get this information from experts.

Scientists have created guidelines to help you figure it out. The **Recommended Dietary Allowances (RDA)** lists the amount of each nutrient most healthy people need in a day. Scientists used that information and other guidelines to create MyPyramid. You can use MyPyramid to find out what diet is right for you.

Visit www.MyPyramid.gov and find the tool called MyPyramid Plan. You can build a food pyramid just for you, based on your age, sex, and how active you are. Use MyPyramid Plan to help you make healthy food choices.

MyPyramid represents health and nutrition guidelines produced by the U.S. government.

Keeping Track

How can you figure out what nutrients are in your favorite canned, frozen, or boxed foods? Each food package has a Nutrition Facts label. This label gives you information to help you make good food choices.

All of the numbers on the Nutrition Facts label are based on one serving of the food. Check the top of the label to see how much of the food equals one serving. It may be one cup of cereal, one tablespoon of peanut butter, or half the can of soup.

The Nutrition Facts label tells you the amount of specific nutrients included in one serving of the food. The label also lists a percent next to each nutrient. For example, the label on this page lists 4% next to vitamin A. This percentage shows how much of the total recommended amount of vitamin A is included in one serving of the food.

Use the Nutrition Facts label to choose foods with low numbers in fats. Choose foods with high numbers in fiber, vitamins, and minerals. Making good food choices helps you stay healthy and perform well.

Nutrition Facts

Serving Size 1 cup (228g)
Servings Per Container 2

Amount Per Serving

Calories 250	Calories from Fat 110

	% Daily Value*
Total Fat 12g	18%
Saturated Fat 3g	15%
Trans Fat 3g	
Cholesterol 30mg	10%
Sodium 470mg	20%
Potassium 700mg	20%
Total Carbohydrate 31g	10%
Dietary Fiber 0g	0%
Sugars 5g	
Protein 5g	

Vitamin A	4%
Vitamin C	2%
Calcium	20%
Iron	4%

* Percent Daily Values are based on a 2,000 calorie diet. Your Daily Values may be higher or lower depending on your calorie needs.

	Calories:	2,000	2,500
Total fat	Less than	65g	80g
Sat fat	Less than	20g	25g
Cholesterol	Less than	300mg	300mg
Sodium	Less than	2,400mg	2,400mg
Total Carbohydrate		300g	375g
Dietary Fiber		25g	30g

A Nutrition Facts label appears on most cans, jars, and boxes of food in your grocery store.

Myth: Eat lots of pasta and bread the day before a race.

Fact: Some carbohydrates provide quick energy. Other carbohydrates provide slow, steady energy. When athletes know the difference, they can improve their performance.

2 Energy to Burn and Build

Carbohydrates, fat, and sometimes protein fuel exercise. Which nutrient or nutrients your body uses depends on the type of exercise you are doing. Sprinting and other short, high-powered activities use mostly carbohydrates. Sports like long-distance running still use carbohydrates for energy, but mostly use fat, as well as some protein.

Taking Control of Your Carbohydrates

Let's talk about **whole-grain** pasta, apples, and bananas. In other words, let's talk about carbohydrates. Carbohydrates are the energy source your body prefers. Your body breaks carbohydrates down into **glucose**, a simple sugar. If you don't have enough glucose, you become tired and slow.

Carbohydrates provide fuel for medium- to high-intensity athletic activities. If enough carbohydrates are stored in your body, they will last about two hours. If you eat snacks with a lot of carbohydrates during exercise, your body will continue to use carbohydrates for longer than two hours.

Once your carbohydrates are used up, your body starts using fat for energy. When your store of fat is used up, you body starts changing protein to glucose. This process will give you energy, but it is not very efficient. So it is important to have a large amount of carbohydrates stored in your body before you begin to exercise.

Energy to Go

Experts recommend that teens get 45 to 65 percent of their calories each day from carbohydrates. Carbohydrates come in three forms: simple carbohydrates, complex carbohy-drates, and fiber.

Simple carbohydrates are quickly broken down into glucose by your body. They give you a quick burst of energy. Fruits and some vegetables, like beets and sweet potatoes, are great sources of carbohydrates. Table sugar gives you that same quick burst, but it causes a sharp drop in energy soon after. Table sugar provides no important nutrients and may cause health problems.

Complex carbohydrates come from starchy foods like corn, bread, and rice. Your body has to work harder to break complex carbohydrates into glucose. That takes time, so complex carbohydrates give you a supply of energy over a longer time. Natural, whole-grain starches like barley and brown rice are packed with vitamins and minerals as well as carbohydrates.

The third form of carbohydrates is fiber. It provides no nutrients, but it is still important. Fiber helps your body break down food. It keeps the glucose in your blood at the right level. It helps your **digestive system** run smoothly. You can get fiber from vegetables, fruits, nuts, seeds, and whole grains.

Three Ways to Create Energy

You race down the track and pass other runners. Where does the energy to move your muscles come from? It comes from **ATP**. ATP is a high-energy **molecule** your body produces using the foods you eat.

Your body has three systems to make ATP. The systems work together, but eventually, one system takes the lead.

- System one is used for the first minute of a fast walk. This system provides the burst of energy you need when you do activities like lifting a weight. The ATP supply lasts about 15 seconds.

- System two provides energy after 15 to 20 seconds of activity. You use this system for activities such as running a 200-meter dash or doing gymnastics. After two minutes, system three takes over.

- System three produces energy that can last for hours. Long-distance runners and cyclists depend on system three.

Carbohydrates, fat, and protein fuel your energy systems. Eating the right amounts of these nutrients will help you perform your best.

Spare the Fat and Drain the Carbohydrates

Whether athletes or couch potatoes, people need to eat the right amount and type of fat for good health. The right type of fat is unsaturated fat. It is found in oils, some fish, nuts, seeds, olives, and avocados. The right amount is about 20 to 30 percent of your total daily calories.

A diet that is too low in fat can be dangerous for an athlete. It can cause you to use up your carbohydrates faster and run out of energy. You will get tired sooner and will not perform as well.

Your muscles' ability to burn fat will improve as you train for your sport. As you increase your fitness, you will still burn more carbohydrates than fat, but fat will be a bigger part of what you use. This helps your body save carbohydrates for that final push.

Weighing In on Proteins

Next to water, protein is the main element in your body. It makes up almost 20 percent of your weight. You need protein to grow, develop, and repair your muscles. Protein also helps keep your **metabolism** working properly. It provides energy when stores of fat and carbohydrates are used up.

When you eat food, such as steak, which contains a lot of protein, your body breaks up the food into many things. One of those things is protein molecules. The protein molecules are broken down further into **amino acids**. Then, the amino acids are arranged into new proteins that your body needs. This system requires 22 different amino acids. Your body can make some of them, but nine amino acids can only come from food.

Counting Up Protein Needs

Unlike carbohydrates, your body cannot store protein. So you need to refill your supply of amino acids daily.

Most Americans eat far more protein than they need to because meat is so plentiful in the United States. An adult male needs about 55 grams (1.9 ounces) of protein each day. An adult female needs about 45 grams (1.6 ounces). The average amount of protein **consumed** by Americans is 100 grams (3.5 ounces) per day.

Some people think that eating large amounts of protein builds muscles. This is not true. Larger muscles and strength come with proper training and recovery periods.

Metric Conversion Chart

You can use the chart below to convert from U.S. measurements to the metric system.

Weight
1 ounce = 28 grams
1/2 pound = 8 ounces = 227 grams
1 pound = 0.45 kilogram
2.2 pounds = 1 kilogram

Liquid Volume
1 teaspoon = 5 milliliters
1 tablespoon = 15 milliliters
1 fluid ounce = 30 milliliters
1 cup = 240 milliliters
1 pint = 480 milliliters
1 quart = 0.95 liter

Length
1/4 inch = 0.6 centimeter
1/2 inch = 1.25 centimeters
1 inch = 2.5 centimeters

Temperature
100°F = 40°C
110°F = 45°C
350°F = 180°C
375°F = 190°C
400°F = 200°C
425°F = 220°C
450°F = 235°C

Some athletes need slightly more protein than people who are not athletes. However, eating too much protein is not recommended for several reasons:

- If you fill your belly with protein, you may not have room for other important nutrients.
- Too much protein increases your need for water. Unless you drink lots of extra water, too, the additional protein can cause **dehydration**.
- Foods that are high in protein, such as red meat and cheese, also have a lot of **saturated fat**. These foods are linked to heart disease.

In the Market for Protein

Protein from animal sources, such as meat, milk, and eggs, contain the nine amino acids you can only get from food. Vegetable sources of protein may lack one or more of these important amino acids. But you can still get them all by combining foods. For example, a meal of brown rice and beans has all the amino acids you need.

Soybeans, however, are different from other plant foods. Like eggs, soybeans provide the nine amino acids needed from food. For vegetarians, foods made with soybeans are an important part of a daily diet.

Different exercises use carbohydrates, fat, and protein in varying amounts at different times. All three of these nutrients eventually are used for energy, so be sure you get them all in order to perform at your best.

Myth: To get the most energy, it doesn't matter when you eat as long as you eat the right foods.

Fact: Timing meals correctly around your event improves your level of energy and recovery.

3 Timing Is (Almost) Everything

One fact is clear after centuries of research into what foods fuel an athlete best: a diet that has all the important nutrients provides plenty of energy for exercise. However, certain foods eaten at certain times help improve an athlete's performance and recovery. The most effective timing of meals is based how the body's digestive system works.

Digesting the Facts

Digestion begins in the mouth with chewing. After food reaches the stomach, it is broken down further into a liquid mixture. After two to four hours, this mixture moves to the small intestine. There, the nutrients become small molecules your body can use. Proteins become amino acids.

Carbohydrates become glucose. Fat becomes fatty acids. They can now be released into the bloodstream to give you energy.

Different foods take different amounts of time to leave your stomach. By understanding how the digestive system works, an athlete can time his or her meals to improve performance.

It is okay to enjoy a large meal three to four hours before exercise. But within two to three hours before exercise, it may be best to choose foods that leave the stomach quickly. It is uncomfortable to exercise with food bouncing around in your belly, and the faster the food moves into the small intestine, the sooner it can be used for energy.

Protein, fat, and foods with a lot of fiber are digested more slowly than carbohydrates and liquids. Drinking water with a meal before exercise is a good idea. Water helps **dilute** the food, making it easier for the stomach to do its work. Liquid meals like smoothies and sports drinks leave the stomach fastest of all.

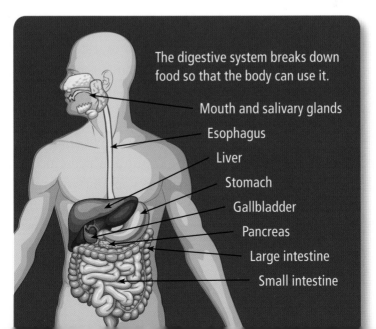

The digestive system breaks down food so that the body can use it.

Mouth and salivary glands
Esophagus
Liver
Stomach
Gallbladder
Pancreas
Large intestine
Small intestine

Loading Up

You could say your pre-exercise menu begins five to six days before the event. Some athletes use a diet plan known as "carbo loading" to increase the stored carbohydrates in their muscles.

On the sixth to the fourth day before the event, the athletes train hard and eat a low-carbohydrate diet. This uses up their stored carbohydrates. Then, the athletes do the opposite on the third to the last day before the event. They train lightly, and they eat a diet high in carbohydrates. Some athletes believe this method increases the carbohydrates stored in their muscles to their highest level.

Sports nutrition experts say that "carbo loading" can cause problems. It may increase your risk of heart disease, **diabetes**, and unwanted weight gain. It may also rob your body of vitamins and minerals and cause muscle loss.

Ahead of the Game

Experts have recommendations about what to eat the day of an event. Eat your last real meal three to four hours before the event. It should include enough food to prevent hunger during exercise, but not too much to digest. Remember, only food that has been absorbed through the small intestine fuels the body. Anything that is still in your stomach at game time will not do you any good.

The meal should include about 70 percent complex carbohydrates and some protein. Too much protein in this meal is wasted calories. It won't give you quick energy, and digesting protein takes more water than breaking down carbohydrates. If your body is processing a lot of protein, you may get dehydrated.

Then, have a snack two to three hours before the event. Keep the snack to between 200 to 400 calories, since there will be little time left for your stomach to process the food. Like the meal before it, make this snack heavy on carbohydrates and light on protein. If your sport involves running or jumping or anything bouncy, you may want to stick with smoothies or yogurt at this point. Liquids leave the stomach fastest.

In the hour or two before the event, take in only liquids. Try a sports drink, or a smoothie if you know your stomach can handle it. Within an hour of the event, water and sports drinks are your best choices.

Let the Games Begin

During exercise, athletes need lots of fluids. Athletes should drink five to eight ounces (148 to 240 ml) every 15 to 20 minutes. Short, high-intensity activities require only water. An athlete needs to replace carbohydrates if exercise goes on for more than 60 minutes. Athletes should eat around 15 to 30 grams (0.5 to 1 ounce) of carbohydrates each half hour.

Liquids or carbohydrate gel packs are good sources of carbohydrates. Some athletes can handle solids during exercise. If so, they should choose foods that have little or no fat or protein. Fat and protein require too much energy to digest.

Athletes who exercise for four hours or longer will need calories. These calories come first from carbohydrates and fat. Protein may be needed at the end of an event for a final burst of energy. When an athlete's stores of carbohydrates and fat are used up, protein will be changed to glucose for energy.

On to Recovery

Once the event ends, it's time to refuel. Drink fluids, no matter what kind of exercise you did. Then, begin replacing carbohydrates. Eat a snack with a lot of carbohydrates within 15 minutes after exercise ends. Try fruit juice or a smoothie.

Within the next two hours, you want to eat a real meal. Get lots of carbohydrates and some protein. During these two hours your body quickly changes carbohydrates into a form that can be stored. Don't wait more than two hours to eat. After two hours your body's ability to store carbohydrates decreases by as much as 50 percent.

What's most important for recovery is a balanced, nutritious diet. Be sure to consume every important nutrient, including vitamins and minerals.

Within two hours after finishing exercise, eat a meal with lots of carbohydrates and some protein.

Myth: When you sweat a lot, drink as much water as you can.

Fact: Humans cannot store water. It's important to drink water before, during, and after exercise.

4 Essential Elements

Carbohydrates, fat, and protein supply energy. Whether they fuel a big competition or just a quick walk, everyone needs them. Another nutrient you need a lot of is water. Water provides no energy, but you need a constant supply of it. Your body needs water to process carbohydrates, fat, and protein. In fact, water is involved in every process connected to nutrition.

Like water, vitamins and minerals provide no energy but are still extremely important. Vitamins and minerals help your body change carbohydrates, protein, and fat into energy. Without them your athletic performance will not reach its highest level.

Fluids First

Everyone loses 6 to 12 cups (1.4 to 2.8 liters) of water every day through urine, feces, breathing, and sweat. Athletes may lose much more. In extreme cases, athletes can sweat out as much as 6 cups (1.4 liters) of water per hour!

Mild dehydration is a loss of 1 to 2 percent of your body's necessary water. It can cause headaches and tiredness. A loss of 3 to 5 percent of your body's water affects your heart. Your body doesn't function well. You may lose concentration and feel extreme thirst or nausea. You may even collapse. If your body's water level drops 10 percent or more, your life may be in danger.

There are six reasons why water is so important:

1. Water dissolves other substances. It dissolves large molecules into smaller substances that your body can use.
2. Water moves things. It carries the small substances through your body to where they are needed. It also moves substances you don't need out of your body.
3. Water reacts with chemicals. It works with chemicals in your body to keep all of your systems operating.
4. Water provides structure to your body parts. From the tiniest cells to your bones and muscles, every part of your body contains water.
5. Water provides protection. It keeps your joints lubricated and your eyeballs moist. Water also provides a cushion for your brain and other body parts.
6. Finally, water keeps your body's temperature at the right level. When your body overheats, you begin to sweat. Water comes out through your skin, taking extra heat with it.

Mixing in the Minerals

When you sweat, you don't lose just water. You also lose **electrolytes**. Electrolytes are minerals that come from the foods you eat. They keep the fluids balanced in your body. They also help your nerves, heart, and muscles work right.

Some people believe that vitamins and minerals are only important when you're growing. In fact, they help change carbohydrates, fat, and protein into energy. Without them your athletic potential won't be reached.

Minerals come from the earth. They are found in soil, rocks, and water. Since the body cannot make minerals, it is your job to put foods with a lot of minerals on your plate every day.

Tricks of the Trade

Here are a few things to know to avoid dehydration:

- Feeling thirsty is your body's way of telling you that you're already low on water. Don't rely on thirst to set your drinking schedule.
- It takes 10 to 20 minutes for fluids to travel from your stomach to your skin. Make sure you have had plenty of water before exercise and sweating begin.
- The stomach can only absorb about one quart (0.95 liters) of fluid per hour, so you can't meet your water needs by gulping down a gallon. Instead, drink water before, during, and after exercise to make sure you are hydrated.
- Choose sports drinks over sodas. Healthy sports drinks contain the right kinds of sugars and some minerals that your body needs.

Boning Up on Calcium

You have more calcium in your body than any other mineral. It is needed for the development of bones and teeth. Calcium also plays a part in other body processes. If you don't get enough calcium as a child, you may suffer a bone disease called **osteoporosis** later in life.

Pumping Iron

We all need iron to produce a protein called **hemoglobin**. Hemoglobin carries oxygen in the blood from the lungs to body tissues. When the iron levels in your blood drop, your body tissues get less oxygen and you get tired. Athletes should get their hemoglobin levels checked each year.

Zinc

Zinc is another important mineral, although you just need a little of it. It helps build a strong **immune system** and is important for building proteins. Without enough zinc, your body becomes less efficient at producing energy during exercise.

Valuable Vitamins

Vitamins are best known for helping the body grow and maintain hair, fingernails, and skin. They also help break down carbohydrates, fat, and protein. Like minerals, they are needed for you to perform your athletic best.

There are 11 vitamins everyone must have. Some are water-soluble, which means they dissolve in water. When you get more water-soluble vitamins than your body needs, the extra is flushed out in your urine. Fat-soluble vitamins dissolve in fat. Any extra fat-soluble vitamins you take in are stored in your body fat.

B-Smart

Not having enough of the necessary vitamins can cause unhealthy side effects or disease. A lack of B vitamins especially seems to weaken athletic performance. These vitamins help release energy from carbohydrates, fat, and protein. A healthy diet gives you the B vitamins you need.

The human body can make only a few vitamins. That means you must eat the right foods to get your vitamins. Fortunately, most foods contain more than one vitamin. A well-balanced diet will meet your vitamin needs.

Too Much of a Good Thing

It is almost impossible to take in dangerous amounts of vitamins and minerals when you only get them from food. However, it is possible to suffer harmful side effects from overdosing on vitamin/mineral dietary supplements.

Eat fruits, vegetables, whole grains, lean protein, and unsaturated fat. Food will meet your nutritional needs whether you are an athlete or just a healthy person.

Vitamins and Minerals	Some Food Sources
Vitamin C	Oranges and grapefruits
Vitamins A, E, and K	Dark green leafy vegetables
B vitamins	Meat, fish, eggs, milk, beans
Iron	Meat, fish, nuts, seeds, spinach
Calcium	Dairy foods, broccoli, salmon
Zinc	Meat, shellfish, dairy foods, whole grains

Myth: Supplements are perfectly safe.

Fact: Some supplements are safe but are not effective. Some are safe only under a doctor's supervision. Others can be life-threatening. Be aware and be careful.

5 Winning the Race with Wisdom

Nutrition is the process of providing your body with all the food necessary for health, energy, and growth. Both the athlete and the couch potato need the same nutrients to live. No matter how active you are, a healthy diet begins with 45 to 65 percent carbohydrates, 20 to 35 percent fat, and 10 to 35 percent protein.

Many athletes have mistaken ideas about nutrition. They may not trust that they will get enough nutrients from food. They may get information from the wrong sources. TV shows, magazine ads, and team members can provide strange definitions of a nutritional diet.

Weighing In on Nutrition

Weight management is a hot topic among athletes. Some athletes try to reach an ideal weight for best performance. Many athletes participate in sports with weight require- ments, such as wrestling. When it comes to losing weight, athletes should stay away from extreme methods.

One common way to cheat weight requirements is to dehydrate yourself before a weigh-in. However, rules have changed in many sports with weight requirements. Athletes who lose more than 1.5 percent of their body weight in one week are disqualified.

Sadly, some athletes try to lose weight through starva- tion. If starving yourself is your way of "getting in shape," you are mistaken. You may even be suffering from a serious eating disorder. You may need professional help.

Athletes who need to bulk up may reach for foods loaded with fat. It's a sure way to gain weight, but it also increases the risk of heart disease and other health problems. If you need to gain weight, make sure you make smart choices about your menu.

Checking into Supplements

Dietary supplements in the United States are a $20 billion-plus industry. There are around 29,000 dietary supplements on the market. The biggest category of supplement sales is "sports-energy and weight-loss." If you're an athlete, you may have used or thought about using sports supplements. Some are sold over the counter. Some require a doctor's prescription. A few can be obtained illegally. They may be sold as vitamins, drugs, and hormones.

Expert Advice

Some sports supplements have been linked to unhealthy side effects. The American Dietetic Association, Dietitians of Canada, and the American College of Sports Medicine advise athletes to be extremely cautious about sports supplements. These organizations recommend that athletes not use sports supplements until they have "discussed the use of the product with a qualified nutrition or health professional." In other words, unless your doctor or nutritionist says it's okay, it's *not* okay!

Experts discourage the use of protein supplements. Protein requirements can easily be met by diet alone. The huge quantities in supplements may cause health risks.

Here is a list of some common supplements that have been linked with unhealthy side affects.

Supplement	Why Athletes Take It	Some Harmful Effects
Anabolic steroids, sometimes called "roids" or "juice"	To build muscles	High blood pressure, heart disease, liver damage, some cancers, stroke, baldness in men, facial hair in women, interrupts normal growth in teens, may even cause death
"Andro" and "DHEA"	Said to build muscles	Similar to effects of anabolic steroids
Human growth hormone	To build muscles	Harms physical development
Creatine	Said to add strength, energy	Muscle cramps, weight gain, diarrhea, kidney failure
Ephedra	Said to increase metabolism and burn fat	Heart disease, stroke, death

Does this mean all supplements are bad? Absolutely not. Some supplements are bad, though, and most are unnecessary if you are eating a healthy, balanced diet.

The makers of sports supplements may make false claims in their ads. Remember, no supplement can give you the powers of a superhero. If it sounds too good to be true, it probably is!

Go to the People Who Know

An athlete's team members, coaches, and trainers are all important people. Their support is extremely helpful. Their advice can take an athlete from good to great. Still, they may not be nutrition experts. Locker room chat is often filled with myths and outdated information that can lead to nutrition disasters.

As an athlete you may want to improve your energy level, or you may want to lose or gain weight. Talk to your doctor first. Before changing your diet, have a complete physical. If nothing is wrong, you may want to take the next step. Speak to a sports **dietitian**.

These sports nutrition experts understand the energy needs of athletes. They can help you choose healthy carbohydrates, good fats, and complete proteins. They can also suggest a variety of tasty foods with all the necessary vitamins and minerals.

This is not to say that a sports nutrition expert is necessary to win. Getting an expert's advice is just one more tool in an athlete's toolbox. You wear the right shoes, follow the best training program, and keep a good attitude. Also eat the right foods—every day—to fuel your body.

Glossary

amino acids: The building blocks that form protein.

ATP: A high-energy molecule called adenosine triphosphate. ATP provides the energy that muscles need to contract.

calorie: A unit of measurement, like an inch or a mile, used to calculate the amount of energy provided by a carbohydrate, fat, or protein.

carbohydrates: Compounds found in sugar and starch. Carbo-hydrates are the main form of energy for the human body.

consumed: Taken in as food or drink.

dehydration: A condition that occurs when the body does not have enough fluids. Dehydration can be mild to severe. It may be caused by not drinking enough water, or by too much sweating, vomiting, or diarrhea.

diabetes: A disease in which the level of blood sugar is too high.

dietitian: A person who is an expert on nutrition.

digestive system: The system in the body that takes in and processes food to gain nutrients and get rid of waste.

dilute: To make a liquid thinner or weaker.

electrolytes: Minerals that the body needs to control fluid levels in the blood, body tissues, and cells.

fiber: Material in plant foods that cannot be digested. Fiber is technically a carbohydrate, but it provides no energy.

glucose: A simple sugar; the body's major source of energy.

hemoglobin: A protein found in the blood that contains iron. It carries oxygen from the lungs to the body tissues.

immune system: The system that protects the body against disease and infection.

metabolism: The chemical processes that provide the energy and nutrients necessary for life.

minerals: Substances from the earth that the body needs in small amounts to remain healthy.

molecule: The smallest part of a substance that has all the characteristics of the substance.

nutrients: Substances needed by the body for energy and tissue-building. The six types of nutrients are carbohydrates, fat, protein, water, vitamins, and minerals.

osteoporosis: A disease in which the bones become increasingly weak and break easily.

protein: Complex substances present in muscles and other parts of the human body.

Recommended Dietary Allowances (RDA): Average amount of nutrients needed daily for most healthy people.

saturated fat: Fat found mostly in meat and dairy foods.

unsaturated fat: Fat that remains liquid at room temperature.

vitamins: Substances the body needs in small amounts in order to process nutrients for energy.

whole-grain: Made with a grain that keeps all of its parts when it is processed into flour.

Find Out More

Books

Clark, Nancy. *Nancy Clark's Sports Nutrition Guidebook*. 4th ed. Champaign, IL: Human Kinetics, 2008.

Litt, Ann. *Fuel for Young Athletes: Essential Foods and Fluids for Future Champions*. Champaign, IL: Human Kinetics, 2004.

Shryer, Donna. *Peak Performance: Sports Nutrition*. New York: Marshall Cavendish, 2008.

Websites

Children's Hospital Boston
http://www.youngwomenshealth.org
http://www.youngmenshealthsite.org

KidsHealth (Nemours Foundation)
http://kidshealth.org

MyPyramid
http://www.mypyramid.gov

The United States Department of Agriculture
http://www.nutrition.gov

Index

Page numbers for photographs and illustrations are in **boldface**.